Free Verse Editions

Edited by Jon Thompson

THE FOREVER NOTES

Ethel Rackin

Parlor Press
Anderson, South Carolina
www.parlorpress.com

Parlor Press LLC, Anderson, South Carolina, 29621

Library of Congress Cataloging-in-Publication Data

Rackin, Ethel.
  [Poems. Selections]
  The forever notes / Ethel Rackin.
      pages cm. -- (Free Verse Editions)
  Poems.
  ISBN 978-1-60235-370-1 (paperback : alk. paper) -- ISBN 978-1-
60235-371-8 (Adobe ebook) -- ISBN 978-1-60235-372-5 (ePub)
  I. Title.
  PS3618.A343F67 2012
  811'.6--dc23
                                    2012039347

Cover design by David Blakesley.
Cover image: © Kiki Smith and Universal Limited Art Editions, Inc.
"*Etc., Etc.*" 1999. Photogravure on mold-made Hanemühle paper and
collaged lithograph and photolithograph on handmade and machine-
made Japanese paper. Digital Image © The Museum of Modern Art/
Licenced by SCALA/Art Resource, NY.

Printed on acid-free paper.

Parlor Press, LLC is an independent publisher of scholarly and trade
titles in print and multimedia formats. This book is available in
paperback and ebook formats from Parlor Press on the World Wide Web
at http://www.parlorpress.com or through online and brick-and-mortar
bookstores. For submission information or to find out about Parlor
Press publications, write to Parlor Press, 3015 Brackenberry Drive,
Anderson, South Carolina, 29621, or email editor@parlorpress.com.

For Dan

Contents

THE FOREVER NOTES

Notes

Meet me in the cabin

Meet me in the sea
Meet me where our love's a shirt
Drenched, dried out, and drenched once more

Relax into the first note of nothing

The sky's becoming
The book's *this too shall follow you erelong*
Because the sun's pink
It's mid-afternoon
There's a possibility you'll live not knowing
The sky's there, fools rush

You lie in a told tree sure

And the books of elders beside it
You lie in a told tree sure
And the books of elders beside it
The books of elders in the told tree
And the books of elders beside it
You lie in a told tree sure
And the books of elders beside it

Let this be an eraser

Let this be a day
Let this book turn inward on wheelbarrows
Whose spokes set sail across the sound
Whose sound grows absent as waves
Let this sound restore the sex in want
And sail across the sound
By the time this reaches you
You will have grown to grieve me
Let the memory of my sound
And the brightness of wheelbarrows
Spell loneliness
A tempest of flowers folds onto fields of delay
And the absence of wanting sets sail
And the dresser stands in abeyance

So far I have this pen

So far I know this tree
That has been changing
Red as a tree
And blue as bark in winter
This tree is neither modernist—
In the cubist style—
Nor does it have any
Symbolic signification
Tree that is ripe for me
Tree with a vine
Tree in its own time

How wonderful to go riding

And to feel the sadness
That loneliness leaves
When it leaves
How wonderful to go riding
To fall into that sadness and know it
The breath of fall and the buds that spring
To experience sales also
In the adrift of language's departments
How wonderful to feel sadness
That springs from summer monuments

The frame of forever is wanting

However soon this thing
Noon is still waiting
It's something to see
As leaves which are for changing
In case of something, I have this case
Today I may be starting
I may be starting
To let go of the exaggerated waiting
Flowers too choose breathing
Choosing breathing, they can breathe!

Where is the tea

And where is that awful waffle bread
Where are the cookies
After all these being fantastic
Fantastic to buy chocolate
In the first place
In the in-between of morning
And the Frank Stella of sadness
How about the aftermath
And the drunkenness
And the morning of aggressive sadness
Where, after all, is that glassiness
Where is that frankness
After all where is the cookie dough
These too being fantastic

Story where I kept you

You and the Avenue of vines
Vines where I kept you
You and the Avenue of vines
You and the Avenue
Vines where I kept you
You and the Avenue of vines
Vines kept stories
Stories where I kept you
You and the Avenue of vines
Vines where I kept you
You where I kept you
Stories and the Avenue
Of vines

It's raining in the forest

It's raining on the sea
I make a whale-like ship
No matter how blighted
Two sticks to fight with
Two sticks to win
I hold onto these sticks
They say rain is coming
Wind in the valleys
Wind in the trees
I tear one for my honey
To fashion a roof to

The rodeo is up

The roads here are deep crevasses
Across the land and in the ditch is music
And in Beverly it's everyone's music but mine
I take the risk—
Adrift in internal music
I lift my place, not placed either
Everybody's shoes suspect suspense

Where should I put my little feet

Where should I put my flower
Now that I'm in clover
Now that I've drawn my fire
The many teenage years
That shed out back beside her

Setting out against trees

A girl's light and the dark of trees
That and the orange flame—
A way is won, the day is done
In this way married to myself
At the same time trees and a fence

When Sepulveda hastens

Pre-in-me circuits pursue
The step-up to the curb
In Sepulveda pursuing
Loss by time and a curb
In circuits waiting
Cars of waiting
And the park of Caesarian pursuing
Men who kick setting-up to the curb
The heavy men and circuits of pursuing
In time for curbs

You and the laborious night of trees

Trees and the night around you
You and the laborious night of trees
Trees and the night around you
Laborious night
You and the trees
Trees and the night around you
You and the laborious, laborious night
Night and the trees around you
You laborious trees
Night and the trees around you

It was a lovely house, really —

The kind you'd spent your summers in
The trees would need pruning
Now that summer was done
A house to be contented in
Now that the ship had been drawn
A picture of a ship
And a mantel to rest it on

The path wreathed in silence

Wrings round branches
And takes dreams down with the ship
Paths of this sort are warnings
Of stories leaving
Since leaves also
In going, go

Night is the time for travelers

Who pass invisibly from trees
For in all our traveling
What have we become?
A river's edge has it
More than a pond
That empties into a rivulet
You cannot expect it

Sleep Song

I want to remember the picture
Wander into the picture
Thread the threads of sheep in the picture
If this were allegory you would come to love me
You would see that sheep are good (though greasy)
You would not need drinking
You would not need pills for your longing
If this were a picture we would live together in the river
Turtles would welcome us in the wide and deep river
We cannot swim because it is dark and we are under water
The sheep are marvelous and have begun to take pictures
We can step inside and become something else entirely
Like a picture of sheep

Pictures

Amanda

There is a small girl named Amanda.
Like me she is small from the start
and has strong allergies to people and conditions.
She wants two shots only I'm afraid to give them to her.
Her father is a reckless genius. Her mother makes the money.
She lives in a tiny room the size of a rowboat.
There are slits for windows that look out on my childhood beach
and a miniature of my cosmetic bag by her bed
with tiny make-up and tinier pills.
Around us is a city. The city is enclosed like a houseboat.
The scenery is so lush I want to run into it and roll around
only I can't because it's scenery
and it would hurt Amanda who is too sick.
I try anyway. I realize I have to move things around
even though I'm in the enclosed city.

On Sundays

I visited the plants in the plant museum.
The idea had come to me to fix a plot for these plants
since my own experiments had proven a greedy attempt
and everything in my garden had rotted or burnt down
to its roots which were questions.
It had been raining a lot in those days
and while some of the plants had thrown out new shoots
others would not grow back
since they had not been cut to the five leaves.
Nevertheless, I waited for them to grow.
They told lies. They confused my birthplace
and claimed a mongoose makes a wonderful pet.
I didn't let on. I thought that by tricking myself
into believing them, I could save their lot.
Sometime later, when things had become truly bleak
with a new kind of disease that turns leaves into lace,
I received an invitation from the plant museum manager.
At first, I welcomed his invitation. The manager was not so sure.
Once disease reaches the stem, the whole thing has to be cut.

Movie Poems

Talk to Her

How can speech be enough in a clinic
that holds no prisoners?
In other words, he cannot talk to her.
He gives her manicures and brings her teacher
to describe the latest moves.
Her face is the face of his mother.
The voice that flies against the windows
of the dance studio across from his apartment.
Meanwhile, there are other dancers—
nightgowns, a trust fall, the speckled red and white flowers
of a lover's betrayal. The female bullfighter is an archetype
of the other man's desires. Eventually he will become the face
of the delusional man in love. They will search for lost lives
in clinic corridors, in dreams of stale photographs,
in an apartment under siege by its neighbor.
Once he has slipped through the cracks
of the story into the vegetative other.

Far From Heaven

A "Chinaman" lamp next to a coral chenille sofa.
At the men's bar he will take his scotch neat.
His wife is the embodiment of a glass breaking
but appearing put together.
The black man is a postcard for a long ago lover
and he must leave this love for Baltimore.
The gayness of the white husband will be revealed
in an office, by a pool, in a hotel room, and finally in love.
The dream of integration is the dream of sex between men
is the dream of the frustrated fifties' housewife
and the black man who plays her gardener.
The children are an afterthought in the lush grounds

though think about them later.
The scene revealed is of an "Oriental" landscape,
a darkly lit cubist painting, and a ritualized form
in red and blue. The hand of the black man in love
with the orange-gloved hand of the white woman.

Lost in Translation

He's an older actor who's selling scotch
in plastic Tokyo. She's a college grad.
They are Americans who meet
in the out-of-place bar of the Park Hyatt.
The attraction takes the form of a video game cab ride,
a drunken karaoke party, and an alliance with jealousy
at a cook-your-own style restaurant.
The kiss on the street is a scene of attachment.
There are his calls to his wife to discuss rug samples,
the cheesy hotel bar singer, and young Japanese friends
who help them fall in love.
Her lipstick is the color of a faded apple.
In the make-do bathroom mirror
her husband, the photographer, is absent.

Facing Windows

It's a wall of nothing, he thinks,
now that he's curating a show on nothing.
The same kid who sang in the choir,
played with indie-rockers, sits in his apartment
in a conversation with a beer he missed in college.
In the afternoon, light hits that wall, creates a triangle.
He writes about money, love, and Godlessness.
The students come—they have every best intention.
They climb the sides of the state building shouting,
We will run our own university!
They watch *La Dolce Vita* in their pajamas
and leave neon freezy-pop juice all over the tables.
Meanwhile, she enters in a middle.
It's long after *The Exorcist.*
"In a Station" was written in the last century.
Stranger to car design, utilitarian function, she thinks,
Prelude to a Kiss or prelude to this poem.

Walking in Asheville

is like being a dog finally let off his leash into a field
of wet dandelions, weeds, and miniature white roses.
The ground beneath is moist, his nose faces the sky,
which is not azure or cracked but simple dimply blue.
It lacks refrain. It lacks undertow.
The girl's face caught in the wind, car radio blaring,
sun coming down hitting each object at an angle.
The wind picks up, a ray is read, the girl's mother's voice
in that instant, *I don't know whether I'm selfish or cruel.*
The surprising tonic of a dog running through an ordinary field.
Though she's passing by, there's her mother letting go—
the glass of brandy shaking on the bedstand in the dark room
with blue carpet. The house in the nice section of town, its paint
stripped down to bare wood. The dog circling the sloped side-yard
beneath her mother's window.

Buttonwood Street

A shoe is found between some dog-eared copies of recipes.
The skeletal remains of animals, a calendar put out by Seed Company.
He wanted to preserve matched lights: SNCF stamped on their fronts.
She didn't care and so on. This much is true:
they walk into the house and the house eats them.
It says, *fix me, water my plants, carve out a space*
for the dreaming book and the one left open in rain.
The couple's love of the house is contagion:
it kills whatever lives inside them.
Each one says, *I need this* and *this is what I can't live without.*
They are in the basement and this house has no basement.
Candles line the driveway. Guests walk through moldy vines.
She has drawn herself into the hill and he is off looking at races.
They have crossed the river of *no* and *yes.* Who's to say they should listen?

Radio Free Europe

In a letter she has written,
You make the Woolworth sign of my childhood come on.
She has not received a letter in return.
It's winter. The blindness is new
but already the exact shape and dimension of things
gets lost. Fog forms damply around her.
She goes to the library of fifteen steps and to the left.
Manuscripts are impossible to decipher.
She tells herself gorgeous ghost stories
involving revolving doors
and checks her astrology report in braille daily.
In the photograph, she's standing with her mother,
back to a storm, arms carrying the weight of what's coming.

Avenue C

The summer after our return, we took up living
around the corner from Key Foods.
The 300 pound man who stood out front
accused you of having a big gut *like me, like me.*
I was standing in a café—was it the same one
I'd been in earlier? Was Benny's still open?
The following fall pigeons purred dirtily
on your fire escape as afternoons slung low
into evenings, naked as cars barreling down C.
I'd ended up waiting at Around the Clock,
an oddly shaped cloak around my shoulders,
until the 6 came to pick me up or the 4 or the 11.

Preserving Jennie

is knowing a sun comes up each morning.
A saucer for drinking and two ceramic cups after you've moved in.
The pine tree and large facing windows in a train station foster thoughts
of others and long lists. If a widow had something she'd give it to Jennie.
Now we are together; Jennie is no more distant. If the moon wallows,
so does Jennie. Then there's this turn-around. The pieces are eventually
woven in.

Museum

They are walking around the small museum
located in a depressed area.
In several corners bulbs have been hung.
Metal flowers with faces like people.
Two paper-maché trees of approximately the same size,
creating a correspondence.
Between them: hay where there would normally be sky.
Two chairs and a catalogue on the objects.
As is customary, each object has a title:
Trees for Henry, Bouquet of Lost Flowers.
In a crypt, her thoughts must be transparent—
His arm. The word *leech*.

Fish Journal I

Take the narrow path down to the underground fish observatory.
Behind plexiglass windows: see tail fins.
Fishes as a group eat nearly anything edible found in or near the water,
    but most are carnivores.
At a burrito stand tell friends about *The Fishes,* but do not mention
    actual fish.
Decide *Fishes Without Jaws* works as a band name.
Both the extinct ostracoderms and their living jawless
    representatives.
Continue reading for phrases to jump out.
Determine to take up the life of the cow-nosed ray, the oceanic skip-
    jack, the blind cavefish.
Fishes rival birds in brilliance, but whereas the color of birds is life-
    less, staining the dead feathers, in fishes it is living and chang-
    ing—the fish changes color when necessary.

Fish Journal II

Red rocks form a canyon gorge.
Juicy birds confirm the word *caw*.
Where elevation is king, a certain fear of altitude.
Take the highway, the quickest route down.
Bike paths lead to other longer paths.
Surprised by a group of blood capillaries, the windpipe, no longer
    needed, is discarded.
Another group of blood capillaries dismisses your bunch as the
    bunching species.
Digits wander across keys, a nurse refuses to let any news pass by.
A straight state in the shape of a woman is not a woman.

A Boat That's a Raft

points toward the Atlantic in the shape of a star.
Its basic shape can be taut, is the song on a piano when played
    slightly flat
so that the side facing a hand is the hand on the face that says
    I'd really rather not.
Then there are those knots on the side of a sculpture born in 1999—
the year of graduation when cake was a substance to sink down into
as garden is wander if you're a wanderer, which you happen to be.

Shapes Form Picnics

Hand on a gun that forms a fan though the gloaming.
You and I step into an ocean not unlike the gap when a hand meets
    a zipper and is undone.
We make lives like this, shape our bodies with bits of distress.
Repeat a thousand times. Tie hammocks to trees. The sense
    of augury gone.
The solid skull resting on its foundation. The femur bone clearly
    attached also.
Of all the things I sent you, this one sealed in a cardboard box.

Songs

What Befalls You

I could no longer stand the trees
when a stand of them began to blossom.
That summer was one of the best.
We were ourselves, miraculously.
All of a sudden fall fell, as fall always does.
Rolls of film went missing, and with them
something less detectable.
Say it was a severe season with the children rushing in
in great strokes of clarity, then years of canceling fog.

My Sister's Drawings of Trees

This red-lined tree with leaves—
where does it come from
where does it go?
Times we play
queen & servant
for a day—
how I wish
it could be different.
A generative act
splits the street
with no trees at all,
still becomes greener.
Flowers that wilt and bloom.
We learn to grow things
like ghosts
we put things away.

A Flower Type

There was a flower type—calendula, say,
or amaryllis—she would come to remember
and pieces of it knit together by Gus
who said her flowers looked like
they had been in the refrigerator
and emerged onto the drawing
and it would take a sister to see
and a mother to face the wall.

Leaflets

There are those whom I need
to be singing
there are those who are singing
so I tear myself—
jealous of silence
and mostly it's whispered
as if by a tree
whose leaves—
shake—
into this telling
into the windy sleep
that strangers inherit
(for they're strangers)
nor did I know
that leaflets burn
or that I'd commence
my life in Erie
O my apostrophized other—

Ode to the River

River, you are long and wide—
a lick away in the mind
and a lick away in time.
Flowing in, you flow out of passion too.
Too injurious to see your own reflection
you are not a narcissistic river and neither am I.
For I have forgiven you and your children,
the rivulets. I have forgiven the mountains
for staying and the birds for taking flight
off the high and middle and lower peaks.
These are mountains in the sense
that you see yourself winding
into rocks and stones and trees.
You keep running
when children scream.
A river of solitude—
one color for me in the sun
and another under the bridge.
Trees against you darken.
Light on you silvers.
Stones fall into you
and crumble white.

~

They come out of you too.
A flag waves by.
People stand and gaze.
The grassy dryness
of not being able.
The sprung roots of a song.
Dissonance reflected in windows
so that looking out creates the kind of dreams
associated with you in the dirt and in the sky.
A tumor appears and on it dreams grow and grow
and grow lake-like and solid. Like a child you climb
and like a creeping vine you weep. Leaves along you

move no matter. What happens in the drunk river of years.
The chicken that limps. A mountain's reflection in you.
Shadows when trees against you bow and gleam.

A Visit

Stone house inland of river's edge
on one of those roads that snakes up
into the hills and mountains
into the arms and valleys
little knot of sleep, tossing
and waking to a dream
of subtraction
while S. dreams
of drawing gymnasts
as she did when she was a girl.

Before Everything

A train leapt into its station
two girls fell in love
two households collided
as dreams that stalked
you haunted me
you whom I have always loved
and held close like a child
and kept afar like little lights
or ghosts across a courtyard
that was before stock quotes
and radiator bleeding
in the songs that we would sing
you whom I have always loved
as an out-of-tune violoncello
as a bird caught on its wing.

Self-Portrait

Your face in a boat of roses
your face in a cloud of stars
your face surrounded by bougainvillea
surrounded by wolves or larks
face of rock-salt or silt: a billion cells or more
one who stares back across a crowded boulevard
baby bougainvillea, your face reflected
one eye looks straight while the other wanders
a night house surrounded by pointed firs
a porch, pleated, beneath ten trillion stars
pulsating bougainvillea
panicking, side-winding stars.

Ode to Stars

O wheels of bright invisible stars
O wheels and stars around them
you bright invisible ones
would not be under cover
if owning were not the blight
it possibly is
or if this shuddering
of ancestors
who quake in their invisible boots
could wake into a day.

Ode to a Lamp

Lamp, you are an enchanting one
a hideous one besides
your tortoiseshell exterior shines
against the stark reason of morning
and complements even the silkiest afternoons
causing one to comment, *how precious*
and another to explain, *I can hardly bear it*
or *I wish it were mine*. The gemstones encrusted
on your shade, supposedly found in catacombs,
are the kind given to mothers. When I leave,
you are still on.

Ode to the Elgin Marbles

When will I be ready to see those great sepulchers?
When will I be ready to see them?
Is there a type of preparedness
I can expect to be transferred?
All the while the marbles are growing
older. They are growing and being seen.
When will I be released into their sight?

No Octave, Mi-Carême

Mi-Carême in song
in some Mi-Carême
me adrift in song
caring for Mi-Carême
a draught of wine
Mi-Carême in song
whether or not in-country
or in a draught
of Mi-Carême's song
no fright Mi-Carême
Mi-Carême my song.

Song

An awfully pleasing song in the branches.
A song that reaches as far as an eye can see.
Despite the annoyances, despite the contrivances,
despite the ridiculous need to sing to be.
The branches' fright when what they sing
is pleasing. As far as an edge,
the need to sing to be.

Ode to the Bereft

In the days that follow
experience disorder
as advantageous crossing
and be courageous enough to do this
whenever you think of me
cross the great stream
the days will follow you
when you think of me, be courageous
imagine a field and experience it
whether or not it may be.

Ode to a Wand

Wand, you are surely one
that will bring wishes
as buoys strung along the bend
of a channel
guide travelers
however far you will fan out
you will fan out
across treetops where there is knowing
and in traffic which brings the world's noise
the world wounds, scraping its tender carapace,
coaxing, while under your sturdy carapace
there is longing
and knowing the trees are real
brings them in a brush of serene noise.

Ode to Birds and Wishes

Birds in the nearest elm
you who knit channels
you whom I would like to meet

feathery birds like you carry wishes
that travel down rivers
and run into the sea.

~

Such wishes float admirably
lining the many notes that she wrote.

~

People are entombed by the sea.

~

Across the wires of rivers
a wireless connection is made.

~

Tune or tomb: song
sung by wandering Carmens
who take cover in beds by the sea.

~

She said she was working on ruins—
I could only imagine
the image of monuments.

~

A wish springs as weather strikes stone.

~

It was not that I missed her,
but I missed her.

~

She wrote the *she* of my dreams.
Did she still live in that cabin?

Press of Days

A blind bird nests in a tree-like hat.
Days emerge stolidly.
What seems like a thousand cranes pass by
only to be remembered
from an earlier landscape
before such grainy, lit interiors.
Night moves like a cloud pierced.
This must be the place.

Acknowledgments

Grateful acknowledgment is made to the following publications, in which poems from *The Forever Notes* first appeared, some in different form: *Big Bridge, Colorado Review, Evergreen Review, Insurance, Kelsey Street Press Blog, MiPOesias: The David Trinidad Edition, Zócalo Public Square.*

A series of poems from Notes, including "You live in a told tree sure," "The frame of forever is wanting," "Story where I kept you," and "You and the laborious night of trees," was set to music and performed by the Norman David Eleventet in Philadelphia in 2011.

The title line of "You live in a told tree sure" is adapted from a line in Gertrude Stein's "Susie Asado." The line "Into rocks and stones and trees" in "The River" is adapted from a line in William Wordsworth's "A slumber did my spirit seal."

For his generous readings and insightful suggestions, I am grateful to Jon Thompson. Thank you to my teachers, colleagues, and friends for their support, including Christopher Bursk, Thomas Devaney, Joan Houlihan, Joanne Leva, James Richardson, Hassen Saker, Susan Stewart, David Trinidad, and Arthur Vogelsang. Love and gratitude to Rebecca Hoenig, Phyllis and Donald Rackin, and Jennifer Schoerke. This book is dedicated to Dan Spirer. Thank you for everything.

About the Author

Ethel Rackin was born in Philadelphia. Her work has appeared in *The Amerian Poetry Review, Colorado Review, Court Green, Evergreen Review, Poetry East, Volt,* and elsewhere. She earned her MFA from Bard College and her PhD from Princeton University. She has taught at Penn State Brandywine, Haverford College, and Bucks County Community College in Pennsylvania, where she is currently an assistant professor.

Photograph of the author by Julie Leva.
Used by permission.

Free Verse Editions

Edited by Jon Thompson

13 ways of happily by Emily Carr
Between the Twilight and the Sky by Jennie Neighbors
Blood Orbits by Ger Killeen
The Bodies by Chris Sindt
The Book of Isaac by Aidan Semmens
Canticle of the Night Path by Jennifer Atkinson
Child in the Road by Cindy Savett
Contrapuntal by Christopher Kondrich
Country Album by James Capozzi
The Curiosities by Brittany Perham
Current by Lisa Fishman
Divination Machine by F. Daniel Rzicznek
Erros by Morgan Lucas Schuldt
The Forever Notes by Ethel Rackin
The Flying House by Dawn-Michelle Baude
Instances: Selected Poems by Jeongrye Choi, translated by Brenda Hillman, Wayne de Fremery, and Jeongrye Choi
A Map of Faring by Peter Riley
Physis by Nicolas Pesque, translated by Cole Swensen
Poems from above the Hill & Selected Work by Ashur Etwebi, translated by Brenda Hillman and Diallah Haidar
The Prison Poems by Miguel Hernández, translated by Michael Smith
Puppet Wardrobe by Daniel Tiffany
Quarry by Carolyn Guinzio
remanence by Boyer Rickel
Signs Following by Ger Killeen
These Beautiful Limits by Thomas Lisk
An Unchanging Blue: Selected Poems 1962–1975 by Rolf Dieter Brinkmann, translated by Mark Terrill
Under the Quick by Molly Bendall
Verge by Morgan Lucas Schuldt
The Wash by Adam Clay
We'll See by George Godeau, translated by Kathleen McGookey
What Stillness Illuminated by Yermiyahu Ahron Taub
Winter Journey [Viaggio d'inverno] by Attilio Bertolucci, translated by Nicholas Benson